The Aquinas Lecture, 1969

BEYOND TRINITY

Under the Auspices of the
Wisconsin-Alpha Chapter of Phi Sigma Tau

By

BERNARD J. COOKE, S.J., S.T.D.

MARQUETTE UNIVERSITY PRESS
MILWAUKEE
1969

231W
C774

79052521

Library of Congress Catalog Number 70-81373

© Copyright 1969
By the Wisconsin-Alpha Chapter
of the Phi Sigma Tau
Marquette University

PRINTED
IN
U.S.A.

Prefatory

The Wisconsin-Alpha Chapter of Phi Sigma Tau, The National Honor Society for Philosophy at Marquette University, each year invites a scholar to deliver a lecture in honor of St. Thomas Aquinas whose feast day is March 7. These lectures are customarily given on the first or second Sunday of March.

The 1969 Aquinas Lecture *Beyond Trinity* was delivered March 2 in the Peter A. Brooks Memorial Union by Rev. Bernard J. Cooke, S.J., Professor and Chairman of the Department of Theology, Marquette University.

Fr. Cooke was born in Norway, Michigan, on May 31, 1922. He earned the A.B. at St. Louis University in 1944 and the M.A. in 1946, the S.T.D. at the *Institut Catholique de Paris* in 1956. He taught Pastoral Theology at the *Grand Seminaire* in Paris in 1955 and 1956.

Fr. Cooke joined the Marquette Faculty in the spring of 1957 and became

Chairman of the Department of Theology in 1958. Under his direction the department developed a full graduate program in Religious Studies.

Fr. Cooke's interest in ecumenism and in reforming the teaching of Theology has extended his influence far beyond Marquette University. In 1960 he was elected to the two-year presidency of the National Society of Catholic College Teachers of Sacred Doctrine and at present is an editorial associate for the new *Journal of Ecumenical Studies*. In the summer of 1967 he lectured in Japan on the Theology of Vatican II.

Fr. Cooke's publications include: *Formation of Faith,* Chicago: Loyola University Press, 1965; *Christian Sacraments and Christian Personality,* New York: Holt, Rinehart and Winston, 1966; *Christian Involvement,* Chicago: Argus, 1966; *New Dimensions in Christian Life,* Wilkes-Barre: Dimension Books, 1968; articles in *The Catholic Mind, Christian Century, Theological Studies, Theology Digest, Ave*

Maria, Perspectives, and *The Modern Schoolman.*

To these publications Phi Sigma Tau is pleased to add: *Beyond Trinity.*

Beyond Trinity

In a 1960 essay that appeared in a *Festschrift* for Bishop Stolz of Mainz,[1] Karl Rahner remarks that there has been practically no instrinsic development of the classic treatise on the Trinity since the Council of Florence. A sad situation, if the judgment is literally true, since it would mean that theology—if it is really that: the study of God—has been static for close to a half millenium. There is much to say for Rahner's negative appraisal, as we will see shortly, but his own article with its suggestions for a "new look" at the theology of the Trinity is one of the indications that something is stirring in theological thought, something deep and far-reaching enough to give promise of a basic reconsideration of our Christian theology.

It is this exciting promise of the most important theological development in centuries, perhaps the most important in the

Church's life up to this point, that I would like to explore with you this afternoon. That something important is happening in Christian theology seems fairly evident: sacramental theology is being radically and quite rapidly rethought in terms of that which is most proper to sacraments, their symbolic reality;[2] a number of elements of Christian existence that were previously studied in somewhat dispersed and artificial isolation from one another are now being integrally studied in what has come to be called "Christian anthropology";[3] theological ecclesiology, rather than canonical classification of Church offices or polemic justification of denominational claims, is coming into its own[4] to the extent of exercising a major influence on Vatican II. But perhaps the clearest indication of the radical nature of today's theological endeavor is the fact that the question of God has come center stage.[5]

Without attaching exaggerated importance to their insights, the so-called "God is dead" theologians[6] are an indication of the fact that the God-question is squarely before us. The Christian theologian has been challenged to explain to our contemporary world the God in whom Christians believe, the God we have pointed to with the term "the Trinity." Obviously, it will not do to repeat unchanged the verbal formulations of the past, particularly if, as is just possible, they are less than totally adequate. The reality of God to which previous generations of Christian faith were directed remains unchanged, but only that reality; theology faces the task of providing an understanding of that object of faith which takes full account of the scientific, historical, critical advances of modern thought. In a previous stage of Christian theology, actually a very early one, the kind of human categorizing that found expression in the word "trinity" helped Christian faith avoid some of the pitfalls of error and superficiality. Recognizing the fact that that element of intelligibility in the notion "trinity" which truly corresponds to the reality of God as known in Christian faith must be preserved in our own present-day reflections, contemporary theologians are nonetheless questioning the extent to which the idea "trinity" corresponds to the reality of God as revealed in Jesus Christ.

It might be worthwhile to point out that theologians are not engaged in dressing up the classic notion of "trinity" in more contemporary terminology, so that Christianity appear relevant to our world.

Nor is it an expression of discontent with Hellenic influence on Christian thought, which in some circles happens to be a favorite "whipping boy."[7] What is at stake is a profoundly serious, even anguished, search to find God; what is at stake is not just the future of theology, but the future of Christian faith and with it the possibility of finding any ultimate meaning for our human existence. The theologian's search to create a less inadequate explanation of the God who has revealed himself is of vital importance to him as a man and as a Christian.

Of course it is also vital to him as a theologian. This is the ultimate test of his methodology, for if he has not the professional tools by which to guarantee the accuracy of his understandings of the divinity he can lay no claim to membership in the scholarly community. Moreover, if his method does not lead to results, to deepened and more fruitful understandings of God, he has nothing to contribute to man's knowledge of himself and his world.

Today's lecture is not a step in the creative work theology must undertake—would that it were! Rather, its purpose is more modest: to indicate how in our present Christian theology there are occurring the early stages of that creation, and to suggest the possibilities for more understanding of the God we love and worship.

Today's theological endeavor can only be understood accurately if it is seen as the latest stage in a centuries-long evolution. This is true, not only because no age can divorce itself from its historical antecedents, but because methodologically the theologian cannot ignore the process of Christian tradition from which he must draw his seminal and normative insights.

The task of trying to find means of expressing in human thought and language the intrinsically ineffable mystery of the divine is essentially the same unavoidable challenge the infant Christian Church faced. Immersed in the shattering experience of the Christ-event, the life and death and resurrection of Jesus of Nazareth, the early Christians tried to give some meaning to this happening and to themselves as a community formed by faith in this happening.

In striving to explain the presence of divinity in Jesus the Christ, the early Church found itself faced, both within and outside the Church itself, with two religious mentalities: to the Jewish world it had to relate the God who raised Jesus from the dead to Yahweh "who brought our fathers out of Egypt"; to the Hellenic world it had to relate the Father of Christ to the ultimate principle and goal of all being. In many respects the relationship to the religious heritage of O.T. Israel was easier to suggest: Yahweh who for centuries had worked salvifically for his people and who in the very works he accomplished for Israel had given promise of an eschatological fulfillment of his saving providence, had now in the death and resurrection of Jesus accomplished this definitive work of salvation. Easter is the "day of the Lord"; it is the establishment of God's kingdom through the mediation of the risen Christ. Yahweh stands revealed, then, as the Father of Jesus who is the Christ, and whom he sends into the world to accomplish its redemption.

So far so good; but who, then, is Jesus? Is it enough to see in him the fulfillment of Israel's Messianic hopes, even if one applies the term "messianic" in its broadest sense, and by applying them to Jesus synthesizes all the various traditions of eschatological hope that are attached to the titles "Son of Man," "Servant," "Son of God," "Messiah," "the great prophet," the synthesis we find in the N.T. literature?[8] Apparently, this did not suffice: the Gospels in particular reflect the insight of Christianity's earliest theologians that Jesus' work of historical fulfillment to

which these various titles pointed was
more than just exaltedly human; instead,
his work, both in its origins and in its
teleology, opened onto the mystery of the
divine. Thus the very titles of Messianic
realization had to be subsumed into something yet greater: Jesus not only proclaimed Yahweh's word as the greatest of
the prophets, he is that very "word" en-
fleshed (Jn. 1). Not only is Jesus the
unique Servant of Yahweh, but through
fidelity to this Servant role and in the supreme exercise of his Servanthood he is
constituted the Lord (Phil. 2). To him
applies the Messianic phrase, "the son of
God," but it has much more far-reaching
implications; he is Son in a most unique
way, for equality with the Father belongs
somehow to him—"All that the Father has
he has given to me" (Mt. 11:27). "I and
the Father are one" (Lk. 10:30). "In the
beginning was the Word; and the Word
was with God; and the Word was God"
(Jn. 1:1).

Clearly, the religious traditions of Israel were of key importance for the under-

standing that early Christianity had of Jesus and his role—they were unquestionably so for Jesus himself in his own human self-understanding; but it would be good to remember that we cannot justifiably fit the Christ-event into categories already established by Judaism. If there is one thing that is clear from the N.T. writings it is the *newness* of what has occurred in Jesus. To formulate an understanding of this new reality men had to fall back upon categories of thought and patterns of expression already in existence; but the understanding they poured into these forms exceeded the forms and gave them new reality. Here the remark of Bernard Lonergan, when discussing the hermeneutical question, is easily applicable: "The great difficulties of interpretation arise when the new wine of literary, scientific and philosophic leaders cannot but be poured into the old bottles of established modes of expression. In such cases the type of expression, so far from providing a sure index to the level of meaning, originally was an impediment which the writer's thought could not shake off and now easily can become a misleading signpost for the unwary interpreter." It was the N.T. itself that first spoke of pouring new wine into old wine skins!

If the theological understandings of Jesus possessed by the N.T. writers and the traditions they reflect are difficult to determine—a difficulty that seems indicated by the divergent views of prominent exegetes—the early Church's understanding of the Spirit is almost beyond recovery. Reading through the N.T. writings we are not even certain whether we should refer to the Spirit as "he" or "it"; the N.T. does both. Unquestionably, we are somewhat aided by the O.T. notion of the "spirit" of Yahweh; the creative, sanctifying, and life-giving power that flowed from Yahweh himself; the spirit that comes to Messiah and to prophet so that they can witness to truth and help bring into being the rule of Yahweh (Isaiah 11, Ezek. 2); the spirit that is so closely allied with Yahweh's presence and glory and wisdom (Ezek. 39:28-9).

Yet, one gets the definite impression that the N.T. literature is drawing essentially from the community's experience when it talks about the Spirit. The Spirit of Christian Pentecost was not known through theological reflection; he was directly though mysteriously experienced in the life of faith and hope and love in which the early Christians shared and by so sharing became the body of Christ (Eph. 2-4). For these primitive Christian communities, possession of the Spirit is inseparable from their prophetic function (Acts 2:14-21), just as was the case with Jesus himself (Lk. 4:16-30); inseparable also from their priestly function, for it is through the Spirit dwelling in their hearts that they can speak the only appropriate Christian word of worship, "Abba, Father" (Rom. 8:15-16).

It is almost inappropriate to ask of the N.T. books: Is the Spirit truly God? Granted, one does have the so-called "trinitarian formulations" of the Pauline doxologies and of Matthew 28:18, which itself reflects at least one current of early

Christian baptismal practice. Yet, the N.T. scarcely raised the question of the onto-logical relationship of the Spirit to the Father and to the Son—his equality or sub-ordination, his derivation or dependence, his co-eternity. All that one can say with some assurance is that the early Church understood the Spirit as belonging both to the immanent life of the Godhead and to the divine economy of salvation that was manifested in Israel, in Jesus, and in the Christian community.

Already in the period of the N.T.'s composition the Christian community had to confront the Greek cast of thought and utilize it to express its faith in the God who revealed himself in Jesus and in the gift of the Spirit. It is still a matter of serious scholarly questioning how much the N.T. expression of Christian faith through Greek language and categories of thought, especially through key words like *logos,* is to be related to current Hellenistic thought and how much to O.T. categories mediated through the Septuagint.[11] How-ever, there was certainly some need to confront Greek ways of thinking; the Epistle to the Colossians seems a rather clear indication of this.[12]

In writings like Colossians one notices a change in the task that the community has undertaken: in relating to Jewish thought the Christian endeavor was essentially one of situating Jesus' activity and the action of the Pentecostal Spirit within the history of Yahweh's salvific activity. Now, in confrontation with Hellenism, the effort must rather be one of situating the Father, Jesus, and the Spirit within the structures of being.[13] Is the Father to be identified with the ultimate One and All, the source and plenitude of unity and being? And if so, where fit in the Son and the Spirit? Are they as ultimate and uncreated as the Father? Is the Father the one God, or do the three somehow constitute this ultimate source of unity? To put it in more imaginative terms, is the Father alone at the top of the ladder of being, or are all three together at the very top?

From the 2nd Century onward the development of Christian theology was an attempt to find a satisfactory response to those questions, with various terms and categories (*ousia, physis, hypostasis, substantia, natura, persona*) being employed to reconcile into some framework of non-contradiction the unity of divine being and the distinctiveness of Father, Son, and Spirit. Modalism, subordinationism, tritheism all arose as possible explanations; all were rejected—at least in their more apparent forms—as a peril to the integral truth of biblical revelation.[14]

Gradually, there emerged the formulations of Nicea and Constantinople, of Ephesus and Chalcedon, credal statements that grew not only out of philosophically theological reflection and polemic refinement, but also out of the more scripturally and experientially based faith confessions of the baptismal and Eucharistic liturgy.[15] One would also misread the credal statements of these great Councils, as also the theological writings of the great Fathers of those centuries if he forgot that they were intended to give clarification and restatement to the faith expressed in the N.T.

However, we must ask if those credal formulations, and the later theology that explicitated them, were not drawing heavily from an intelligibility, a cast of mind, formally distinct from the mentality of the N.T. community. To apply the term *persona* or *hypostasis* to the three who are yet one in their *substantia* or *ousia* does help avoid the pitfalls of error; but by virtue of its abstract formalizing it also has the disadvantage of suggesting a certain homogeneity: all three are persons, all three are subsistent relations. Of course, one can distinguish Son from Father as the begotten from the unbegotten; but even this was done to bolster the divine equality of the Son rather than to indicate his positive distinctiveness—except by way of opposition: he is *not* the Father.[16]

The tendency of Latin patristic thought, observable already in Tertullian[17] and maturely operative in Augustine,[18] to begin with the divine unity in nature does help avoid tritheism. But it has its own dangers, which did not fail to materialize in later Christian theology and spirituality. The divine nature comes to be viewed as an infinite neutrality untouched by trinity; divine being is practically a prior-given reality which the three persons possess in common, the Father possessing it un- received, the Son from the Father, the Spirit from both. When one reads the *Monologium* of Anselm (presented for the prayerful contemplation of his monks![19]) or studies the treatise *De deo uno* which from Thomas Aquinas onward is so neatly distinguished from *De deo trino,* one feels oneself in a thought world quite other than that of John's Gospel or the Epistle to the Ephesians.

This is not to question the value and need in Christian thought of careful philo- sophic reflection about the transcendent, if for no other reason than to preserve faith from excessive anthropomorphism and idolatry. But one must ask whether the revelation of Father, Son and Spirit can then be fitted into the formalities of thought set up by such reflection; are we not thereby in danger of neglecting the radical "newness" of Christian revelation? And is there not even danger, as some passages in Abelard's *Introductio ad theologiam*[20] suggest, of a subtle modalism creeping into discussion of the trinity?

While it does not run the same perils, Greek patristic emphasis on the three persons and their inter-relationship develops into the same notional abstractness. Already in the theology of the great Cappadocians this is pretty well crystallized; and it remains an unmodified heritage of both East and West down to our own day. Gregory of Nazianzen speaks explicitly of "processions" and sees the unbegottenness of the Father as his distinctive characteristic.[21] Gregory of Nyssa speaks of the distinction of persons as relative.[22] Augustine adopts these Cappadocian insights, combines them with his utilization of psychological analogies and his insistence on the unity of divine nature as starting-point —and much of the essential framework for our classic treatise on the trinity is already in existence.

But at this point one wonders what

has happened to the N.T. basis for distinguishing the Father, Jesus, and their
Spirit. Have we not moved into another
realm of discussion, one of principles of being and structured natures and abstractly-
formulated relations? Is not, for example,
the Word (who, at least according to the
N.T., is Jesus) looked at as the principle
of intelligible manifestation of inexpressi-
ble creative unity, rather than as the Father's manifestation of his loving and saving self-gift to men? This seems to be the
case as far back as Clement of Alexandria
—before the year 200.[23] Does not the inner
life of God become an object of esoteric
theological reflection, cut off from the
work of salvation in which we are involved
and with which we are concerned? Certainly the principle introduced by Gregory
of Nyssa, passed on with approval by
Augustine, and with scarcely a challenge
cherished by theologians up to our own
day[24]—the principle, namely, that the distinction of persons applies only to the
inner life of God and that in all activity
"ad extra" the three persons act as one—

has meant that the work of creation, including even the level of "grace," can give us no proper insight into the personal distinctiveness of Father, Son, and Spirit. And our appetite to know the Father, who has loved us enough to reveal himself in Jesus, has been fed with the thin gruel of a theory of appropriation.

Is this not, however, much too harsh an evaluation? Can one legitimately make the historical judgment that the centuries-long adventure in trinitarian thought deviated from the guidelines of revelation provided in Scripture? Obviously, such a statement is too simple and too sweeping. When the Greek Fathers draw upon the notions of *gennetos* and *agennetos,* to distinguish Father and Son, they are certainly not unaffected by the N.T. usage of these names, "father," "son." Admittedly, it is more difficult to see how the word "procession" *(ekporeusis)* as used by the Cappadocians for the Spirit[25] draws its intelligible content from the scriptural idea of "spirit." The Greek Fathers were clearly intrigued and influenced by the mystery of the divine Logos described in the prologue of John's Gospel. But, again, one wonders to what extent they assigned the Word the tasks of the Platonic *logos* rather than concentrating on the function the Word performed as incarnated in Jesus of Nazareth. Certainly Augustine drew deeply from the Bible when he explained the Word and the Spirit from both cosmic and psychological perspectives; but one cannot avoid a lurking suspicion about the relative ease with which Augustine can read the biblical Father, Word and Spirit into the neo-Platonic One, Mind, and Spirit.[26]

Augustine's use of psychological analogues in his justly famous *De trinitate* had, as is well known, a far-reaching effect on all future development of Western theology. Thomas Aquinas made his own modification of Augustine's approach; but it seems that he used essentially the same method: taking human spiritual reality as his starting point, and seeing it as a unique image of divine personal existence, he used the human person's self-expression through knowing and loving to provide insight into the divine processions of Word and Spirit.[27] Obviously, in doing so, he is under no illusion that one can argue from the created realities of human psychological life to the nature or even the possibility of a triune God. But given, through revelation, the truth that God the Father does express himself in his Word and in his Spirit, one can proceed to shed light on this mystery by seeing some vestige of these immanent divine relationships in the complex unity of human consciousness.

Admittedly, however, such refined speculation can give no proper insight into the triune life of the Godhead—as St. Thomas says in the *Prima Pars,* "the creative power of God is common to the whole Trinity, whence it pertains to the unity of and not to the distinction of persons. Through natural reason man can know those things about God that pertain to the unity of essence, not those that pertain to the distinction of persons."[28] This kind of reasoning permits the theologian to show that there is no clear contradiction in the dogmatic formulations of trinitarian belief. It also permits him to ascribe certain titles or attributes more appropriately, though not properly, to one divine person rather than to another—as, for example, "power" to the Father.[29]

As a matter of fact, the great mediaeval treatises on the Trinity are an impressive display of metaphysical and psychological insight and of complicated deductive reasoning. Person, relationship, procession, nature, origin, mission, all are delicately and accurately brought to bear on the terms, Father, Son, Word, Spirit, Gift that are drawn from Christian revelation. And all this is done without any peril to the attributes of eternity, immutability, unity, simplicity, or infinity that are proper to the divine essence. So masterful was the systematizing of trinitarian thought in the thirteenth century, particularly by Thomas Aquinas, that for many centuries there seemed to be no point in doing other than repeat it.

Today's discontent with the remoteness and abstractness of this synthesis should not lead us to neglect its great

value. Christian faith accepts the revealed
"names of God" as true symbols, even
though inadequate symbols, of the reality
that is the immanent life of God. In ex-
ploiting the intelligibility of these names,
patristic and mediaeval theology was providing understanding of the God who reveals himself.[30] Cannot we today incorporate this wealth of insight into an understanding that begins not with divine
names, but with those more immediate
and concrete symbols: the living faith of
the Christian community?

While this carefully structured treatise
on the Trinity prevailed for centuries, practically untouched except for differing philosophical interpretations of "subsistence,"
as this applied to person or nature, an iso-
lated voice now and then began to raise
questions. Petavius with his pioneering
work in positive theology,[31] Maldonatus
before him[32] and Thomassinus[33] shortly
after, prepared for Scheeben's challenge
to the adequacy of classic trinitarian theology, particularly to the neglect of the divine missions.[34] For decades the insights

of Scheeben remained unexploited, looked
upon by most theologians as interesting
speculation that lay outside the main-
stream of Catholic thought. All that has
now changed; Scheeben's most original
insights are seen as steps in the right direction, contemporary theology has drawn
from them and gone beyond, and we face
the prospect of fashioning a theology of
the God of Christianity that will respect
all the valid insights of classic trinitarian
theology but not be confined to the de-
limiting logic of its abstract formulations.

Many forces have fed into this recog-
nition of the need to reconsider our theology. Perhaps most importantly, modern
study of the Bible, with its insistence on a
careful critical search for the literal understanding of the scriptural statements about
God, has revealed a tension between the
outlook of the scriptural writers and that
of systematic trinitarian theology. To give
one example of this: It is well-nigh impossible to read the N.T. and come away with
the view of a God who in his creative
work "ad extra" reveals nothing of his own

immanent life. This seems to negate the very notion of a God who reveals *himself* in his salvific deeds. On the contrary, the N.T. speaks of a God who creates all things in and through his Word and by the power of his Spirit; all creation bears the mark of Christ; and the ultimate life force working in man, and therefore in the universe, is God's own life-giving Spirit.

Scriptural categories have, then, challenged the adequacy of Hellenic thought patterns; a challenge that finds a partial resonance in modern philosophical, scientific, and psychological thought, which has increasingly evolved away from the rather tightly-structured categories of Greek philosophy. One must, obviously, move carefully in making such judgments: it is somewhat fashionable today to stress the advantages of de-Hellenization; but it would be foolish impoverishment of our own understanding to reject the irreplaceable contributions Greek thought has made to our own knowledge of man and his world, and historical nonsense to deny the extent to which even our most contemporary thinking has evolved out of the Greek heritage. Moreover, the history of Christian theology—which unfortunately still remains to be written—would reveal the way in which the faith and life of Christians have deeply transformed the categories of Greco-Roman thought that Christianity employed to understand itself. Thomas Aquinas' radical transposition of Plato's and Aristotle's most focal insights is but one indication, though probably the most important, that Hellenic thought was not taken over unchanged as the matrix for Christian theology.[35] Yet, there is no doubt that modern thought has shifted from a structured analysis of natures which themselves embody necessary and unchanging truth, to a more functional and evolutionary way of thinking; process and history, relativity and contingency and induction, have assumed increasing importance. Modern theology long held itself aloof from this new cast of mind, at least in part because it misunderstood the nature of Christian tradition and its own role in the process;[36] but this is no longer the case.

One striking instance of the present openness of Christian theology to the challenges of modern thought, particularly the challenge to rigid criticism of thought itself, is the preoccupation with epistemological questions. Nothing is more discussed today in theological circles, both Catholic and Protestant, than the hermeneutical issue.[37] Not only is the scientific methodology of theology under scrutiny, but the nature of theology's unique starting point, the act of Christian faith, is undergoing unprecedented study—from the vantage point of several diverse disciples of knowledge. All of this is raising the question of the validity, accuracy, even the possibility, of our knowing some transcendent reality called the Trinity.

Of a different order, but not less important, is the influence of the basic experience of Christians today. Along with their non-Christian contemporaries they are aware of the increasing emphasis in today's world on the human person, on his

dignity and freedom and uniqueness. Thus
there is a richer base of understanding
from which to proceed in applying an
analogy of person to a study of God.
Again, a Christian today shares the contemporary impatience with knowledge
that has no relevance for life; and the doctrine of the Trinity as it was classically
presented seems to most men and women
to have little bearing on their view of life,
or even on their prayer. Yet, if for a moment I can interject an element of the
personal, it has been my experience that
no discussion arouses more interest in a
classroom than an attempt to understand
the deeper religious meaning of the revelation of God as Father, Son and Spirit.
Perhaps this is partially the result of what
is an element of experience proper to
Christians, that of Eucharistic worship.
While we are still a long way from the
meaningful Eucharistic liturgy we truly
need, the liturgical revival of the past few
decades is a force to be reckoned with in
Christian thought. To the extent that Eucharist is celebrated authentically it forces

Christian faith and prayer into a true trinitarian pattern: for Eucharist is the community's uniting with the risen Christ in acknowledgement of the Father through the Spirit. It is a striking exemplification of the old dictum, *"Lex orandi, lex credendi."*

These, then, are some of the influences that have made a reappraisal of our theology of God unavoidable. Certainly there are many others, perhaps equally important as the ones we have mentioned, but these few suggestions may at least indicate that our discussion today is inseparably linked with the principal developments in present-day Christian faith and life. Actually, it is the most radical development, though inchoate; step by step we have been forced to bring our cherished understandings of Christianity into painful confrontation with reality, to appraise critically the verbal and institutional formulations we had given our faith; we have had to re-examine our entire process of religious formation, our understandings of the Sacraments and the life of grace they are meant to foster; we have had to broaden our conception of the Church; this in turn has meant that we had to take a more careful look at the manner in which we think about Christ himself; now we have been driven back to the ultimate reality of our faith, this God who reveals himself in Jesus. But the question then arises: Where do we go from here?

In the remainder of this essay I hope to indicate where contemporary theology is already going in the formulation of a rather new understanding of the God of Christian revelation. To attribute specifically each detail of what follows to the theologian from whom it is derived is impossible, and the attribution might even be an unjustified misunderstanding; but anyone familiar with the theological literature of the past quarter century will recognize the sources of the theological procedure that is here suggested.[38]

Christian theology is an attempt to give intelligibility to the revelation of God in Jesus who is the Christ. While this description is not new, there is one aspect of it that is looked upon somewhat differently today: the process of revelation. Instead of something that occurred centuries ago and resulted in a body of truth that has been handed to us as a completed reality, revelation is now seen to be a continuing process—God still reveals himself to men through his Word and his Spirit. There is a truth in the dictum that revelation ended with the end of the apostolic age; but this has been quite generally and falsely understood to mean that God stopped revealing himself when the last Apostle died. Granting a special role to the faith experience of these biblical communities and to the inspired record of that experience in the Bible, we must still say that the Christian experience of faith today is a present encounter with a God who gives himself salvifically in self-revelation.

However, Christians believe that something unprecedented and unparalleled in the process of revelation occurred in Jesus of Nazareth, and that this occurrence is normative for our understanding of the

revelation that still comes to us through
the risen Christ. With the incarnation of
the Word in Jesus an absolutely unique
avenue to knowing God comes into existence: this man knows the Father in such
immediacy that he gradually discovers
therein his own personal identity as the
Son. This discovery deepens throughout
the earthly career of Jesus and bursts into
full realization with his passage into risen
life.

Many people, and for a variety of rea-
sons, still feel uneasy when this mattter of
the developing consciousness of Jesus is
raised.[40] For some, the uneasiness is
grounded in technical questions of biblical hermeneutics; we will have to deal
with these questions a little later. For
others, the traditional belief in the divinity
of Christ seems threatened by the suggestion that Jesus actually progressed humanly in his discovery of his personal identity.
In answer to these fears, one can appeal
to the implications of Chalceden's formulation of faith in Christ, and specifically
to its solidly traditional insistence on the

fact that Christ was and is truly man.[41]

To be man is more than an abstract possession of "human nature." It is to exist and to act in a certain manner: as we men exist and act. It means to experience in the context of bodily involvement with space and time, above all to experience and discover gradually one's own selfhood. At the very core of this dynamic reality, which is what "being man" is all about, lies the process of "individuation," the progressive experienced activity of discovering and asserting oneself as a person, distinct from and yet related to other persons. For us men this can only take place within the concrete circumstances of a given life situation, a given reality we must accept and to which we must respond. In so responding by consciousness and responsibility and freedom, each man discovers who he is and decides who he will be.

To deny such a progression in self-understanding to any man would be tantamount to denying his genuine humanity. So, it seems that we cannot deny it to Jesus

of Nazareth who was fully man. Moreover, it seems hard to see how Christianity
could propose Jesus as an exemplar of human activity, if he never possessed the
most central and controlling element of
human experience. Such argumentation
is, of course, a bit a priori; but when one
looks to the New Testament for what we
might for the moment call "factual evidence," the evidence does seem to point
quite clearly to a development of Jesus'
self-understanding.

Immediately, however, the objection
is raised: If Jesus did not know the full
divine dimensions of his personal identity
until the resurrection, this means that he
did not know that he was God and therefore he did not know who he was. In response I would suggest that this is a false
formulation of the problem, one that reflects the abstractness into which our
thinking about the "trinity" has drifted.
Even now, in the full light of risen consciousness, Christ does not personally
identify himself as "God." His personal
identify is that of "the Son"; and this iden-

tity is polarized by the person who is the Father, not by the divine nature as such. New Testament texts indicate that Jesus' consciousness of himself and of all else was dominated by his awareness of this person he addressed with the familiar "Abba, Father." His identification of himself was in relationship to this person, his every act and decision was in terms of fidelity to this relationship.[42] His human consciousness, to the extent that its developing capabilities could do so, translated his divine identity of Son. Jesus did know who he is, the son of this person who is his Father; and as his human life unfolded amid the experiences common to mankind, he realized increasingly the implications of this unique relationship, until the full significance broke upon his human consciousness with his entry into risen life.

What this says is that even prior to resurrection, the human consciousness of Jesus stood uniquely exposed to the Father's self-communication.[43] Jesus knew his Father as no one else before or since could know him, not by difference of degree but by qualitative difference. Surely as a thoroughly dedicated Jew he knew his Father in terms of all the religious categories that formed the faith heritage of Israel, because he was a man living in a definite cultural context his understanding of his Father was shaped by this particularized manner of viewing God. As a matter of fact, the continuity of Jesus' own consciousness with the faith of Israel is the deepest aspect of the relationship between the two covenants. Yet, running through all Jesus' Jewish religious understanding, indeed through all his categorized understanding of reality, ran this other intimate and immediate awareness of his Father and of himself in relation to the Father, just as in the consciousness of each one of us the awareness we have of ourselves permeates all our perception of reality and makes the experience of each of us distinctive and incapable of exact duplication.

Already in the O.T. the charismatic prophet's experience of God's self-communication represents a radically new level of divine presence and divine self-revelation. Now in Jesus who is the fulfillment of prophecy, the God of O.T. revelation makes himself present in absolute and constant immediacy to the consciousness of a man. The consciousness that Jesus had of his Father is the supreme manifestation of God in human history, the most direct insight possessed by man into the reality of God, the source of all our Christian understanding of God as personal.[44] Christ himself tells us about this person he knows, an "other" he himself is not, but in relationship to whom he knows himself. Thus, for Christian faith God the Father is not in the first instance the prime analogate of fatherhood, but "the Father of our Lord, Jesus Christ." God the Father is known analogously by analogous attribution of the qualities we associate with fatherhood, but he is known properly as the term of an historically existent personal relationship.

If this be true, the human consciousness of Jesus that was expressed in his words and actions is of indispensable im-

portance in any genuine theological study
of God. To the extent that we can understand what Jesus' experience of his Father
was (and is) we can gain deeper insight
into the divine as it is. If we can in no way
draw from that unique presence of the
Father to human consciousness, it seems
that we are left with nothing more than
very subtle extrapolations from the insights into our ordinary human experience
which philosophy can provide, or with
personal religious experiences we might
have individually or corporately. It is not
our purpose to denigrate either of these
two; but only to point out that if there is
nothing more than this, there is nothing
radically distinctive about Christian revelation, Jesus is not properly God's own
Word to men, and modalism is the only
sensible approach to what we have called
the mystery of the Trinity.

Christian faith does believe, however,
that Jesus was the Word incarnated. If one
takes this matter of incarnation seriously,
it does not mean that in some mysterious
fashion, which man cannot explore, the

second person of the Trinity united himself to this humanity, assumed this individual instance of human nature to himself. It means that this man Jesus of Nazareth, is the Father's own proper Word
spoken humanly so that men might receive
the gift of the Father himself.[45] The function of "word" in any context is to estab-
lish communication through mutual understanding; this is pre-eminently verified
in the case of God's own word—he is the
light that is the life of men (Jn 1:4), sent
because the Father so loved men (Jn.
3:16), sent to bear witness to the truth
that will liberate men (Jn. 8:32).

In telling us that God the Father's own
divine Son is his Word, Christian revelation is pointing to the mysterious fact that
the Father images forth his own identity
in this Son who is his total self-expression
(Col. 1:15). It is this Word, who expresses
his fatherhood even in the inner life of the
Godhead, whom the Father speaks to men
in Jesus. This man Jesus, who himself is
uniquely for all other men at the same
time that he is totally oriented to his

Father, reveals in himself the correlative facts that God is for men and that man in the deepest reaches of his existence is a being for God.[46]

One could go on at great length to discuss the manner in which this man performs humanly the role of the divine Word, drawing from important present-day study of the role of symbolism in human knowledge and specifically in religious faith. However, there is just one aspect of this that I would like to mention, because I think it bears on the hermeneutical question that we will have to confront in just a moment. If Christian theology is to proceed profitably and realistically from Christ's role as human symbol of the divine,[47] and such a procedure seems to promise rich results in our understanding of God, then it is critically important that we know as fully and correctly as possible the historical reality that Jesus of Nazareth was. It was Jesus himself who in his human life and death sacramentalized his Father; but how can we know what that

historical reality is meant to say to us if
we cannot know what that reality was?

It is the basic pattern of biblical revelation that the salvific presence of God is
made known to certain prophetic figures,
and through them to a community of believers, in the concrete milieu of historical
happenings. So, too, the supreme revelation that is made to this man Jesus took
place in conjunction with the occurrences
that made up his historical experience.
Hence, if we are to understand with any
kind of accuracy what it meant for him to
know his Father, and so have this as a
starting point for our theological study of
the inner life of God, it seems important
to know something about this historical
life experience that was his. I am not suggesting that we must become involved in
some fruitless task of trying to recapture
the reality of the historical Jesus, sharply
distinguished from the Christ of faith; but
suggesting rather that the Christ of faith
is in great measure knowable to us because of men's experience of him in the
years prior to his resurrection, an experi-

ence which, illumined by their faith in the
resurrection, they can convey to us.

Hence, then, it seems that we come
face to face with the hermeneutical question as it touches the starting point of
Christian theology we have suggested:
What attempt do we make, and with what
hope of success, to get at the historical
reality and particularly the human consciousness of Christ?

If by one's hermeneutical stance we
mean the principles which govern him in
his interpretation of the biblical texts[48]—
and specifically in this case the texts of the
N.T.—the criteria by which he judges the
validity of his own or others' exegetical
efforts; then it seems to me that we must
bear in mind a basic distinction in these
principles. Some of these are the basic
principles of all scholarly study of literature;[49] but others are more ideological and
many of them are the kind of presupposi-
tions whose presence in his reasoning and
research even the most objective of scholars has difficulty recognizing.

In our present question these ideological stances, which cover the whole spectrum of belief and unbelief, to say nothing of a wide range of philosophical attitudes,[50] are uniquely important. If I, for example, believe that Jesus did actually pass into risen life and that I now stand in familiar relationship to him, and if I believe that this faith of mine is basically the same as that cherished by the early Christians who produced the N.T. literature, then my own religious experience of Christ inevitably flows into my understanding of the mentality that is expressed in the N.T. texts. Now, I may be in error in believing this way—many exegetes would so judge. But if I am not, then I obviously have a vantage point from which to grasp more accurately the original meaning of the N.T. texts. Moreover, if I am correct in this judgment of faith, my interpretation of a given N.T. text is actually more correct than if I divorced myself from my faith in the exegetical endeavor.

Of course, on the presumption that one is working in rigidly scholarly fashion, one

is free to espouse one or other of those
opposed ideological positions only so long
as it is not denied by the historical and
textual study that forms the other portion
of one's hermeneutic. If careful literary
analysis of the N.T. made it clear that
"resurrection" is just a mythic device the
early Christians used to enunciate their
insight into the special value of Jesus'
death, then my belief in a now existent
risen Christ is not congruent with the faith
of the early Christians and, if applied to
the understanding of N.T. texts, would be
a falsifying influence. On the other hand,
if the interpretation of early Christian
statements about "resurrection" as mythic
creation were based on ideological pre-
suppositions rather than on clear textual
indications, it would just as surely be ten-
dentious.

To return, then, to today's specific
question: Is there any purpose to be served
in trying to know the historical realities of
Jesus' life and especially his human consciousness?[51] I think I have already indicated my value judgement in this regard:

if such knowledge be possible, and to the extent that it is, an epistemological medium for knowing the inner life of God is open to us. But is it possible to get at the historical reality of Jesus of Nazareth?

Obviously, there is no hope of recapturing that reality exactly as it was. No one of us can even recall his own past experiences with adequacy or complete accuracy. Moreover, the early disciples of Jesus when they remembered what they had seen him do and heard him say were quite obviously under the influence of their later experience of Jesus as risen. Hence, the N.T. texts witness to a community's faith in the risen Christ and to its attempt to understand that mystery of his Passover from death to newness of life by reflection on what he had said and done previously. The description of Jesus of Nazareth is, then, one that is given by a believing community as it tries to understand more deeply his significance, and therefore its own *raison d'être* as a religious community.[52]

This limitation, that we can contact directly only the literary statements of the early Church authors and not those of Jesus himself,[53] might seem seriously to screen the historical Jesus from our knowledge; and it is just possible that what we have in the N.T. texts is the combination of religious extrapolation and mythic imagination. After all, we do have instances of such religious projection in some of the other religious literature that mankind has produced.

At this point I think that one has to take a hard-headed look at the concrete particularities of the early Christian communities and the production of their sacred writings. The heart of the kerygma, as well as of the catechesis that developed out of it, was "Jesus is Messiah and Lord"; he is the Gospel. Therefore the early Church found itself trying to understand and explain *him;* it was not bent on retaining religious or ethical insights by giving them dramatic form in some creatively imaginative "public life of Jesus of Nazareth." Moreover, the earliest Christians were still very much in continuity with the Jewish heritage of faith in which God was seen as

revealing himself in *events*. Unquestionably the early Church was trying to puzzle
over the deeper meaning of the life and
death of Jesus; but they were trying to
understand the life and death that had
happened, not to replace it with some
other creation of their own. Again, the
early Christian cult—so distinctive in nature that one almost hesitates to use the
word "cult" for it—was historical in an unprecedented fashion. The Passover happening of Christ remained with them as
an ever-present event, into which new
Christians were inserted by baptism (Rom.
6:3-11) and which the community celebrated in its "breaking of the bread" (1
Cor. 11:23-6). This was commemoration
that was much more than recollection; the
present moment was seen as continuing
what had broken forth into history, the
resurrection of Christ. But this resurrection itself, i.e., the risen Christ, was the
fulfillment of the human life of Jesus that
had led up to and prepared it, and as itself a trans-historical reality the risen life
of Christ could not be known to men apart

from the developments of which it was the
outcome. So, it seems logical that the early
Church, trying to explain its faith in the
risen Christ, would have been constrained
to draw as accurately as possible from its
recollections of the actual historical happenings of Jesus' life. The early Church
had a strongly vested interest in safeguard-
ing the key insights and expressions of the
"historical Jesus."

Certainly this is not to advocate a naive
fundamentalism in approaching the Gospels, nor is it a suggestion that one neglect
the various types of critical analysis that
have been developed so painstakingly and
utilized so profitably by exegetes these
past decades. It is only to insist that
though the N.T. writings are a witness of
faith, reflect the faith recollection of the
community, and express understanding
that is grounded in faith, the faith in question is a belief that something happened:
that Jesus of Nazareth lived, taught,
worked wonders, suffered, died, and rose
from the dead (Acts 2:22-34). It seems,
then, that within their theological per-

spective the Gospel writers did intend to relate what Jesus did do and say.[54]

If we are to proceed in theology as I have been suggesting, going beyond the somewhat abstracted analysis that has formed our classic theology of trinity, drawing rather from the human understanding of Jesus as the Son in intimate confrontation with the Father, we must undertake the admittedly difficult task of searching the N.T. texts for contact with the historical reality of Jesus. Yet, such exegesis is not the starting point for our theology. Rather, theology's starting point is the living faith of the Christian community in which the theologian shares.[55]

This faith is the experienced response to God's self-revealing word. Scripture is indispensably normative in understanding the experience of God's word; but the Bible itself becomes fully "word of God" only when it is proclaimed to a community of believers. Because no two Christians, no two Christian communities, are totally alike, the "word of God" that is actually communicated is never quite the same; the

inspired text of the Bible serves in this situation to provide a criterion for funda-
mental unity of faith and understanding,
unity among believers now and unity of
believers throughout the Church's history.
The experience of hearing the scriptural
expression of the word of God, the sacramental experience of enacting the very
mystery of which scripture speaks, the experience of confronting the realities of
daily life with the vision of Christian faith
and hope, all interact to interpret one another and to help fashion that matrix of
personal understanding into which God's
self-revealing presence is received.[56]

God's revelation takes place within the
consciousness of the believers to whom he
reveals himself. Epistemologically, the
Christian theologian must begin with
the shared faith that presently fashions
Christians into a community. But he must
draw from the present faith as something
shared with previous generations of Christians and growing out of their faith. This
takes on added significance if one accepts
in faith the function of the Church as Sac-

rament of Christ,[57] if he sees the faith and
life of the Christian people as giving expression to the present consciousness of
the risen Christ. In this perspective, both
the careful exegesis of the texts of the N.T.
and his educated understanding of the
Church's present faith put the theologian
in some contact with "the mind of Christ."
Inevitably this leads us to the mystery of
the Spirit.[58] Jesus himself comes to a full
realization of his relation to the Father
with his resurrection and complete possession of and by his Father's Spirit (1 Cor.
15:45). So fully does he possess this
Spirit that he can share it with the Church
(Acts 2:33) and thereby share with the
Church that knowledge of the Father that
he himself has in the Spirit. Moreover,
this same Spirit is the expression of the
risen Christ's relation to the Father, and
derivatively of the Christian community's
expression of its filial identity (Gal. 4:6).

It is this same Spirit that the early
Christians experienced as the very atmo-
sphere of their life of shared faith and
hope and love. The Spirit of Christ bound

them together in a community of outlook
and missionary energy. Their knowledge
of this Spirit was not one of categorized
thought, nor derived from doctrinal formulations; rather it was a corporately con-
scious involvement in a new level of human life and awareness. The Spirit is
neither the risen Christ nor the Father;
but it is in this Spirit that the early Christians know the revealing presence both of
the risen Christ and of the Father (Rom.
8:15-15).

   To proceed theologically with the
question, who or what is this Spirit, is a
very delicate task. The Spirit is not identi-
cal with the faith consciousness of the
early Christian communities, yet as known
in faith he is inseparable from that consciousness. Even to use the term "person"
of the Spirit can be misleading, for there
is the danger of using the category "person" generically and thinking of him as
being person like the Father or the Son is
person. To expect intelligibility of the
Spirit comparable to that we have of the
Word through his incarnation is futile, for

the Spirit is not the Word and so could not manifest the Father sacramentally in incarnation.[59]

Rather, it seems that we must, as far as is possible, allow the immediate experience of the infant Christian Church, the experience of being under the domination of the Spirit, speak to us through the pages of the N.T. literature. Then we must refuse to reduce this concrete understanding to categorized concepts.

Again, however, valuable and normative though this biblical source of understanding the Spirit is, it is not exclusive nor even primary. Pentecost is a lasting reality in Christian life; at least this is what the Christian theologian believes. This means that the same Spirit is still active, vitalizing the faith and life of the Church today. Nor need we look for manifestations of the Spirit's presence only in those specially charismatic gifts that are sometimes appealed to as evidence that the Spirit is still with us. The entire experience of the Church, insofar as it is an experience of faith, is a share in the Spirit; by examining the dynamics that are operative in its own corporate awareness and activity, the Christian community should be able to discover the presence of the Spirit.

Thus, the living Church is the principal evidence from which the theologian must work in trying to give some understanding about the Spirit, for the Christian people's unity in love and faith in the risen Christ results from the "mission" of the Spirit.[60] In our classic trinitarian theology we have spoken of the mission of the Spirit as the created extension of his divine procession;[61] but we have done practically nothing to utilize this statement as an epistemological principle. Instead, we have relegated the mention of "missions" to the very end of the treatise on the Trinity, hurriedly discussing this all-important element as if it were almost an afterthought.[62] When someone like Scheeben did point to its importance,[63] theologians were most reluctant to admit that any proper understanding of the Spirit could be gained by this avenue.

Eastern Orthodoxy preserved a richer

tradition of pneumatology than did Western thought and emphasized the role of
the Spirit much more than did Latin theology and liturgy. Consequently, there is
a great deal that we can learn from Lossky,
Bulgakov and other great modern Orthodox theologians.[64] But even here, precisely
because of their devotion to the Greek
Fathers and their drawing from this preci-
ous resource, they still seem to reflect the
"heavenly isolation" of the divine persons
from human affairs that characterizes the
anti-Arian reaction of the patristic period.
At least for the present, however, a theologian whose own roots lie in the Latin
tradition must be careful about judging
this other heritage of Christian theology;
our cultural worlds are disparate enough
to make it necessary to do a good deal of
careful listening before criticizing.[65]

In any event, it seems increasingly
clear that our theological insights into the
reality of the Spirit must begin with our
own experience of faith and life in the
Church; we must learn to listen for the
presence and movement of this Spirit. Ul-

timately this will be inseparable from our
historical studies, for the most basic theological objective in these studies is to discover the Christian faith experience of
past centuries and reflected in it the action
of the Spirit.[66] This is really not so new,
except perhaps to our systematized theology of the Trinity. Christian mysticism of
the most orthodox and profound kind has
long advocated a careful "discernment of
the Spirit" as a guide for Christian decision,[67] but it is interesting that the ability
to discern the Spirit is more an art than a
science. And if we are able, through such
a theological phenomenology, to gain a
deepened knowledge of the Spirit's reality
in the Church, we must be careful that we
do not hasten to force this knowledge into
more comfortable but distorting categories.

This does not mean that we must settle
for a vague and uncritical feeling or in-
tuition. There is the opportunity and the
need for a broad-based and methodologically careful effort of investigation, one in
which contemporary psychology, sociol-

ogy, philosophy are all brought to bear on the concrete religious phenomenon of Christian experience in order to purify and extend faith's consciousness of the action of the Spirit, and therefore of the Spirit's own identity. Theology must also employ the "analogy of faith" by which one aspect of divine revelation throws light on others,[68] and draw from a sharpened understanding of Father and Son, since the Spirit is their Spirit in whom they find incomparable personal expression of their union with and distinction from one another. Even this, however, must remain within the context of the theologian's experience of Christian faith, for that is his methodological starting-point. In proportion as this theological clarification of the Spirit's reality takes place, our understanding of Father and Son will grow, for it is in the Spirit that we not only know about but personally know the risen Lord and his Father who is also ours (Jn. 14:26).

For the most part our discussion up to this point has been aimed at suggesting a theological approach to God as revealed

in Christ and in the Spirit that will safe-
guard the true distinctiveness of Father,
Son and Spirit and provide some insight
into the positive intelligibility of that distinctiveness. We have employed the term
"person" and must unavoidably do so, but
hopefully we have indicated that this word
should be used of Father, Son and Spirit
with full awareness of the analogous nature of this predication, therefore with
stress on the radical distinctiveness of
"person," not just differentiating divine
from human personhood, but distinguishing the reality of personhood as it applies
to Father, Son and Spirit.

This still leaves for our study the reality of divine unity, lest the emphasis on
distinction suggest a latent tritheism. Certainly, there can be no rejection of the traditional teaching about the unicity of divine nature, but perhaps today we can
move another step away from a static conception of divine being and gain further
insight into the dynamic aspect of divine
unity. It seems that a judicious application of the analogy of personal existence,

coupled with what we have already discussed regarding the distinctiveness of the
three divine persons, can provide some
valid insight.

Certainly, the psychological analogies
of Augustine, especially as these were refined by Thomas Aquinas, are already a
valuable entry into some understanding of
the dynamic nature of divine relationships.[69] And one need only read Rahner's
article on symbol[70] or Lonergan's work on
the Verbum[71] to realize that this approach
can still prove fruitful. This analysis pro-
ceeds, however, on the analogy of an individual's consciousness. Another avenue
is suggested by our increased modern insight into the social dimension of personal
existence, into the unavoidable inter-de-
pendence of individual and community,
into the manner in which community is
established by personal self-giving.[72] Is it
not possible to think of the divine being
as being constantly "constituted" by the
dynamic personal communion of Father
and Son in the Spirit? This would be the
ideal realization of that total union in

being towards which our human love vain-
ly strives, but towards which it points.
Community of persons, rather than unity
in nature, would then be our approach
to thinking about the unity of being in
the Godhead.

There are some decided advantages to
this approach: for one thing it is much
easier to give some understanding to the
mystery of man's transformation by
"grace" if we see this as a matter of in-
vitation to share in the divine community,
through personal acceptance in friendship,
rather than as some mysterious "participa-
tion in the divine nature." What emerges
as an exciting view of reality is that the
basic energy of all existence is a thrust
towards community of persons, expressed
primordially in divine community, extended in the mystery of divine graciousness
to incorporate humans into this community, and constituting thereby the intrinsic
principle of mankind's own unification.
This does not simply mean that the historical realities of human community provide an analogy for grasping the mystery

of divine communion; it means that faith can see the Spirit at work to achieve this human unity as the created extension of the dynamism of divine being itself.

The theologian's experience of sharing in the Spirit-constituted community of faith can, then, flow directly into his attempts to understand the reality of God revealing himself in Christ. In such a perspective, ecclesiology and Christian anthropology form an intrinsic and indispensable part of any theological understanding of what we have for many centuries called "the trinity"—and vice versa. Which is just another way of saying that all Christian theology should be just that: theo-logy, an attempt to gain some understanding of the God who has revealed himself in Jesus who is the Christ. Such a theology can never afford to divorce itself from life, from the involvement of Christians in the world as they strive to give expression to their faith in the risen Christ, from the Christian community's profession of its faith in the death and resurrection of Christ through Eucharistic celebration, for it is in this living experience of faith, which the theologian shares with his fellow Christians, that the revealing presence of Father, Son and Spirit is manifested.

NOTES

1. "Some Remarks on the Dogmatic Treatise 'De Trinitate,'" in *Theological Investigations,* vol. 4 (trans. K. Smyth, Baltimore: Helicon, 1966, pp. 77-102); originally published in *Universitas* (1960).

2. Cf. M. O'Connell, "New Perspectives in Sacramental Theology," *Worship,* 39 (1965): 195-206.

3. Not only is this bringing together elements of "dogmatic theology" (grace, sin, creation, etc.), but also much that had previously been separated off as moral and ascetical theology.

4. The most extensive and probably most influential contribution to ecclesiology prior to Vatican II was that of Yves Congar, in books such as his *Vraie et fausse reforme dans l'Eglise* (*Unam Sanctam* 20, 1950) and *Jalons pour une théologie du laicat* (*Unam Sanctam* 23, 1954). Since the Council the most important book is Hans Kung's, *The Church* (New York: Sheed and Ward, 1968).

5. It is interesting to note that much of the ferment leading up to present theological concern for the question occurred in circles that would ordinarily be considered philosophical or literary rather than theological. Cf. J. Collins, *God in Modern Philosophy* (Chicago: Regnery, 1959); C. Moeller, *Littérature du XXe siècle et christianisme, I, Silence de Dieu* (Tournai: Casterman, 1953).

6. Cf. A. Dulles, "Some Recent Death-of-God Literature," *Theological Studies,* 28 (1967): 111-118.

7. One of the more noticed expressions of this cry for "de-Hellenization" was Leslie Dewart's *The Future of Belief* (New York: Herder and Herder, 1966).

8. On the application of these titles to Jesus, cf. V. Taylor, *The Names of Jesus,* (New York: St. Martin's, 1953); O. Cullmann, *Christology of the New Testament,* (London: SMC, 1959).

9. B. Lonergan, *Insight,* (London: Longmans, Green, 1957): 572-73.

10. For a recent attempt to study the N.T. view of the Spirit, cf. J. Massingberd Ford, "Holy Spirit in the New Testament," *Commonweal,* 89 (1968): 173-179. A more technical study is that of E. Schweizer in Kittel's *Theologisches Wörterbuch zum Neuen Testament,* vol. 6, pp. 394-449.

11. Contrast, for example, the strong option of W. D. Davies, *Paul and Rabbinic Judaism,* (London: S.P.C.K., 1955), in his conclusions, pp. 321-324, for the Jewish context of Paul's thought; and the position of W. Schmithals, *Die Gnosis in Korinth,* (Göttingen: Vandenhoeck and Ruprecht, 1965), who emphasizes the influence of Gnostic understandings, particularly of anthropological terms.

12. The Epistle to the Colossians seems to be dealing with some amalgam of Jewish and

Hellenistic or near-Eastern mystic thought, rather than with Greek philosophical thought as such. Cf. F. Bruce, *New International Commentary, Ephesians and Colossians,* (1957), pp. 165-169; also H. Gabathuler, *Jesus Christus. Haupt der Kirche—Haupt der Welt,* (Zürich: Zwinge: V., 1965).

13. An excellent introduction to the question of the shift from the scriptural mentality to that of Hellenic philosophy is provided by John Courtney Murray, in the second chapter ("The Nicene Problem") of his *The Problem of God,* (New Haven: Yale U., 1964).

14. For a detailed review of these developments leading up to the great 4th and 5th century Councils, cf. J. N. D. Kelly, *Early Christian Doctrines,* (New York: Harper, 1960).

15. On the influence of baptismal and Eucharistic liturgy on the development of the early creeds, cf. J. Jungmann, *The Early Liturgy,* (Notre Dame: U. of Notre Dame, 1959): 74-96.

16. Cf. J. N. D. Kelly, *op. cit.,* pp. 231-237.

17. *Adversus Praxean,* 2-3 (CSEL, 47): 228-231.

18. In sketching the plan of his *De Trinitate* (I, 2, 4), Augustine says: "Quapropter adiuvante Domino Deo nostro suscipiemus et eam ipsam quam flagitant, quantum possumus, reddere rationem, quod Trinitas sit unus et solus et verus Deus, et quam recte Pater et Filius et Spiritus sanctus unius eiusdemque

substantiae vel essentiae dicatur, credatur, intelligatur. . . ."
19. "Quidam fratres saepe me studioseque precati sunt, ut quaedam, quae illis de meditanda divinitatis essentia et quibusdam aliis huiusmodi meditationi cohaerentibus usitato sermone colloquendo protuleram, sub quodam eis meditationis exemplo describerem." Anselm, *Opera Omnia* (edit F. S. Schmitt), vol. 1, p. 7.
20. "Clarum itaque, ex supra positis arbitror testimoniis, divinam, ut diximus, potentiam vocabulo Patris exprimi, divinam sapientiam Filium intelligi, ac divinae gratiae bonitatem Spiritum sanctum appellari." *Petri Abaelardi, Introductio ad theologiam* (P.L. 178:998).
21. *Orat.* 23, 7-8 (P.G. 35:1157).
22. *Orat. catech.*, 3, 1-2 (P.G. 45:17).
23. Cf. Sister Melinda Marie Johanning, *The Notion of "Son" in Clement of Alexandria* (unpublished doctoral dissertation, Marquette University).
24. Gregory of Nyssa, *Quod non sunt tres dii,* P.G. 45:125; Augustine, *De trinitate* 5, 13, 14 (P.L. 42:920). Cf. Thomas Aquinas, *Summa theologiae*, I, 32, 1.
25. Cf. Gregory Nazienzen, *Orat.* 31, 9 (P.G. 36:141).
26. Cf. e.g. *Conf.* 7, 9, 13 (P.L. 41:350); on relation of Augustine's idea of God and creation to that of Neo-Platonism, cf. E. Gilson, *The Christian Philosophy of St. Augustine,*

(New York: Random House, 1960), pp. 106-111.

27. *Summa theologiae*, I, qq. 34-38. On the psychological method of Augustine, the classic work is still that of M. Schmaus, *Die psychologische Trinitätslehre des hl. Augustinus*, (Munich: Aschendorffsche, 1927). See also O. du Roy, *L'intelligence de la foi en la Trinité selon saint Augustin*, (Paris: Etudes Augustiniennes, 1966), particularly pp. 400-466, where he traces the evolution of Augustine's thought, indicates the influences on it, and points out Augustine's own special insights.

28. *Summa theologiae*, I, 32, 1. One must not judge Thomas' approach to trinitarian theology on the *Summa* alone; there is a slightly different approach in the *Contra Gentiles* and his commentary on John's Gospel, though even in this latter (cf. *In Joannem Evangelistam Expositio*, chap. 1, 1; cols. 676-682 in Vives edition) his method seems to be the one of working from the analogue of the human act of knowing.

29. Cf. *Summa theologiae*, I, 39, 7-8.

30. The treatment of the question of "the names of God," as handed on to mediaeval thought by Boethius and Pseudo-Dionysius, is contained not only in his commentaries on these two men, but also in *Summa theologiae*, I, 13. Here, however, there is question of the names attached to the divine nature. It is in later questions (33-38) that the problem of apply-

ing names to the three persons is studied.

31. Cf. *Dictionnaire de theologie catholique,* vol. 12, cols. 1313-1337; especially cols. 1334-1336.

32. Cf. *ibid.,* vol. 9, cols. 1772-1775.

33. Cf. *ibid.,* vol. 15, cols. 787-823; especially cols. 799-801.

34. M. Scheeben, *The Mysteries of Christianity* (English trans. by C. Vollert, St. Louis: B. Herder, 1946).

35. Cf. R. Henle, *Saint Thomas and Platonism,* (The Hague: Nijhoff, 1965); E. Gilson, *Le Thomisme* (5th edit., Paris: Vrin, 1947) pp. 15-16.

36. On the nature and role of theology, cf. G. Van Ackeren, "Theology," *The New Catholic Encyclopedia,* vol. 14, pp. 39-49.

37. On the evolution of the modern hermeneutical discussion cf. K. Grobel, "Interpretation", vol. 2 of *Interpreter's Dictionary of the Bible* (1962), pp. 718-724; and K. Stendahl's article on "Biblical theology" in vol. 1 of the same work, pp. 418-432.

38. The re-assessment of trinitarian theology has by no means been limited to Roman Catholic theologians. In Protestant theology one immediately thinks of monumental works like Barth's *Dogmatik* or Tillich's *Systematic Theology;* but others, like Richard Niebuhr, in his article "The Doctrine of the Trinity and the Unity of the Church," *Theology Today,* 3 (1946): 371-384, have raised the question

quite sharply. A very recent instance is Regin Prenter's *Creation and Redemption* (1967). No less important are some of the developments in Orthodox theology which Thomas Hopko describes in "Holy Spirit in Orthodox Theology and Life," *Commonweal* 89 (1968): 186-191.

39. Cf. G. Moran, *Theology of Revelation* (New York: Herder and Herder, 1966).

40. On discussion regarding the human consciousness of Christ, cf. E. Gutwenger, "The Problem of Christ's Knowledge," *Who is Jesus of Nazareth?* (vol. 11 of Concilium), pp. 91-105; also K. Rahner, *Theological Investigations,* (vol. 5, trans. K. Kruger, Baltimore: Helicon, 1966), pp. 91-105.

41. Cf. I. Ortiz de Urbana, "Das Glaubenssymbol von Chalkedon," pp. 389-418 in vol. 1 of *Das Konzil von Chalkedon* (edit. Grillmeier and Bacht, Würburg; Echter, 1951).

42. "I do not seek my own will, but the will of him who sent me" (Jn. 5:30). "I do always the things that please him" (Jn. 8:29).

43. Cf. K. Rahner, "The Enfleshment of God," pp. 97-113 in *Spiritual Exercises,* (trans. K. Baker, New York: Herder and Herder, 1965).

44. If one is to take seriously the N.T. texts that stress the unique mediatorial role of Christ (e.g. 1 Tim. 2:5—"For there is one God, and there is one mediator between God and men, the man Christ Jesus . . .") it would seem that this functions also epistemologically.

45. Jn. 17:3-8.

46. Cf. K. Rahner, *Theological Investigations,* vol. 4, pp. 116-117.

47. Perhaps the most profound treatment of this topic in recent literature is K. Rahner's essay on "Theology of Symbol" in *Theological Investigations,* vol. 4, pp. 221-252.

48. Some idea of the contemporary discussion of biblical hermeneutics can be gained from *The New Hermeneutic* (vol. 2 of *New Frontiers in Theology,* edited by J. Robinson and J. Cobb, New York: Harpers, 1968), though it deals only with the thought of Protestant scholars.

49. On basic notions of hermeneutics, cf. B. Lonergan, *Insight,* pp. 586-594; also V. Hamm, *Language, Truth and Poetry,* (Milwaukee: Marquette U., 1960).

50. Cf. W. O. Martin, *Metaphysics and Ideology,* (Milwaukee: Marquette U., 1959). On the need for various denominations to examine their hermeneutical position vis-a-vis the New Testament, cf. J. Robinson, "A Critical Inquiry into the Bases of Confessional Hermeneutics," *Journal for Ecumenical Studies,* 3 (1966): 36-56.

51. In this regard E. Käsemann makes some interesting observations in his *Essays on New Testament Themes,* (Naperville: Allenson, 1964) pp. 45-47, where he points out both the difficulty and the need of dealing with the problem of the historical Jesus. It might be

good to point out, however, that theological endeavor that is grounded in belief that the faith of the N.T. community was Spirit-guided can accept the witness of that community and can proceed on that basis without being blocked methodolically by the problem of "the historical Jesus."

52. Cf. A. Dulles, "Jesus of History and Christ of Faith," *Commonweal* 87 (1967): 225-232.

53. However, it might be good to remark that in instances where we quite clearly do not have exact citations we may still have a substantially objective recollection of what Jesus actually said.

54. "Inasmuch as many have undertaken to compile a narrative of the things which have been accomplished among us, just as they were delivered to us by those who from the beginning were eyewitnesses and ministers of the word, it seemed good to me also . . . to write an orderly account. . . ." (Lk. 1:1-3).

55. This is something other than beginning with the formulations of its faith that the Church now uses. In his study of Thomas Aquinas' notion of theology, *Sacra Doctrina*, (Rome: Catholic Book Agency, 1952), G. Van Ackeren indicates the possibility of understanding Thomas' approach in this more dynamic sense.

56. Cf. G. Ebeling, "Word of God and Hermeneutic," *The New Hermeneutic* (edit. J. Robinson and J. Cobb, 1964), pp. 78-110.

57. Cf. O. Semmelroth, *Die Kirche als Ursakrament*, (Freiburg: Herder, 1953); K. Rahner, *The Church and the Sacraments*, (New York: Herder and Herder, 1963).

58. See the special issue of *Commonweal*, *(Commonweal Papers: 3, Holy Spirit)* 89 (1968): 173-220.

59. On Incarnation as proper to the Word of God, cf. K. Rahner, *Theological Investigations*, vol. 4, p. 236.

60. Cf. M. Scheeben, *op. cit.*, pp. 149-180.

61. Thomas Aquinas, *Summa theologiae*, I, 43, 1-2.

62. In his *Divinarum personarum conceptio analogica*, (2nd edit., Rome: Gregoriana, 1959), pp. 23-24, B. Lonergan justifies the location of discussion on the divine missions at the end of the treatise by distinguishing between the *via analytica* (the way of discovery) and the *via synthetica* (the way of exposition). But this seems to be just the point at issue: Has not the position of the missions at the end of the treatise betrayed the fact that one was proceeding as if all the previously treated matter could be understood without the missions as a starting-point of intelligibility?

63. M. Scheeben, *op. cit.*, pp. 149-180.

64. Cf. T. Hopko, "Holy Spirit in Orthodox Theology and Life," *Commonweal* 89 (1968): 186-192.

65. Much the same has to be said about Ro-

man Catholic attitudes to and understanding of the Protestant "Spirit" Churches. Cf. M. Novak, "The Free Churches and the Roman Church," *Journal for Ecumenical Studies,* 2 (1965): 426-447.

66. An interesting case for Church history being itself an integral part of ecclesiology is made by H. Jedin in the general introduction to the *Handbook of Church History,* (New York: Herder and Herder) that he and J. Dolan are editing: vol. 1 (1965), pp. 1-10.

67. One of the most famous and widely-used instances is the "Discernment of Spirits" in the *Spiritual Exercises* of St. Ignatius Loyola. The principles enuntiated by Ignatius actually constitute a basic theory of spiritual guidance.

68. Scheeben's *Mysteries of Christianity* and E. Mersch's *Theology of the Mystical Body* are excellent examples of the fruitfulness of this method.

69. Cf. *Summa theologiae,* I, 34-36.

70. *Theological Investigations,* vol. 4, pp. 221-252.

71. *Verbum: Word and Idea in Aquinas* (edit. Burrell, Notre Dame: U. of Notre Dame, 1967); originally appeared as a series of articles, from 1946-1949, in *Theological Studies.*

72. A number of the short essays in R. Johann, *Building the Human,* (New York: Herder and Herder, 1968) deal with this relation between person and community.

The Aquinas Lectures

Published by the Marquette University Press
Milwaukee, Wisconsin 53233

Cicero in the Courtroom of St. Thomas Aquinas
(1945) by E. K. Rand, Ph.D., Litt.D., LL.D.,
(1871-1945) Pope professor of Latin, *emeritus*, Harvard University.

St. Thomas and Epistemology (1946) by Louis-Marie Regis, O.P., Th.L., Ph.D., director of the Albert the Great Institute of Mediaeval Studies, University of Montreal.

St. Thomas and the Greek Moralists (1947, Spring) by Vernon J. Bourke, Ph.D., professor of philosophy, St. Louis University, St. Louis, Missouri.

History of Philosophy and Philosophical Education (1947, Fall) by Étienne Gilson of the *Académie française*, director of studies and professor of the history of Mediaeval philosophy, Pontifical Institute of Mediaeval Studies, Toronto.

The Natural Desire for God (1948) by William R. O'Connor, S.T.L., Ph.D., former professor of dogmatic theology, St. Joseph's Seminary, Dunwoodie, N.Y.

St. Thomas and the World State (1949) by Robert M. Hutchins, former Chancellor of the University of Chicago, president of the Fund for the Republic.

Method in Metaphysics (1950) by Robert J. Henle, S.J., Ph.D., academic vice-president, St. Louis University, St. Louis, Missouri.

Wisdom and Love in St. Thomas Aquinas (1951) by Étienne Gilson of the *Académie française*, director of studies and professor of the history of Mediaeval philosophy, Pontifical Institute of Mediaeval Studies, Toronto.

The Good in Existential Metaphysics (1952) by Elizabeth G. Salmon, Ph.D., professor of philosophy in the graduate school, Fordham University.

St. Thomas and the Object of Geometry (1953) by Vincent Edward Smith, Ph.D., director, Philosophy of Science Institute, St. John's University.

Realism and Nominalism Revisited (1954) by Henry Veatch, Ph.D., professor and chairman of the department of philosophy, Northwestern University.

Imprudence in St. Thomas Aquinas (1955) by Charles J. O'Neil, Ph.D., professor of philosophy, Villanova University.

The Truth That Frees (1956) by Gerard Smith, S.J., Ph.D., professor of philosophy, Marquette University.

St. Thomas and the Future of Metaphysics (1957) by Joseph Owens, C.Ss.R., Ph.D., professor of philosophy, Pontifical Institute of Mediaeval Studies, Toronto.

Thomas and the Physics of 1958: A Confrontation (1958) by Henry Margenau, Ph.D., Eugene Higgins professor of physics and natural philosophy, Yale University.

Metaphysics and Ideology (1959) by Wm. Oliver Martin, Ph.D., professor of philosophy, University of Rhode Island.

Language, Truth and Poetry (1960) by Victor M. Hamm, Ph.D., professor of English, Marquette University.

Metaphysics and Historicity (1961) by Emil L. Fackenheim, Ph.D., professor of philosophy, University of Toronto.

The Lure of Wisdom (1962) by James D. Collins, Ph.D., professor of philosophy, St. Louis University.

Religion and Art (1963) by Paul Weiss, Ph.D. Sterling professor of philosophy, Yale University.

St. Thomas and Philosophy (1964) by Anton C. Pegis, Ph.D., professor of philosophy, Pontifical Institute of Mediaeval Studies, Toronto.

The University In Process (1965) by John O. Riedl, Ph.D., dean of faculty, Queensboro Community College.

The Pragmatic Meaning of God (1966) by Robert O. Johann, S.J., associate professor of philosophy, Fordham University.

Religion and Empiricism (1967) by John E. Smith, Ph.D., professor of philosophy, Yale University.

The Subject (1968) by Bernard Lonergan, S.J., S.T.D., professor of Dogmatic Theory, Regis College, Ontario and Gregorian University, Rome.

Uniform format, cover and binding.